BLACK WOMEN: BRINGING IT ALL BACK HOME

MARGARET PRESCOD-ROBERTS & NORMA STEELE

INTRODUCTION BY SOLVEIG FRANCIS

NORTH AMERICAN AFTERWORD
BY WILMETTE BROWN

FALLING WALL PRESS

Published by Falling Wall Press for Housewives in Dialogue
First published, March 1980

'Until women have spoken . . . ' ©1980 Solveig Francis
'We're in Britain for the money' ©1980 Norma Steele
'Bringing it all back home'.©1980 Margaret Prescod-Roberts
'We come from another field' ©1980 Wilmette Brown

Designed and typeset by Falling Wall Press
Cover designed by John Morton
Printed by Castle Camelot Printers, Bristol
Bound by W.H. Ware & Sons Ltd., Clevedon

ISBN 0 905046 16 1 (cased)
ISBN 0 905046 09 9 (paper)

Falling Wall Press Ltd.
9 Lawford Street, Old Market, Bristol BS2 0DH, England

CONTENTS

TEACHER LEAVES FOR U.S. JOB

Mrs. Elsa Prescod, former assistant head mistress of Christ Church Girls' School, has left for the United States where she will take up a teaching appointment. She was accompanied by her son, **Peter** and her two daughters, **Margaret** and **Vickie**. Mrs. Prescod has been teaching for 13 years and will live with relatives in Long Island.

Barbados Advocate, 2 August, 1961

MARGARET PRESCOD-ROBERTS
LEAVING BARBADOS

INTRODUCTION

UNTIL WOMEN HAVE SPOKEN...

Every day thousands of families leave their native home to look for a better life elsewhere. The result is a continuous international movement of people. It is a very personal experience but one that is shared by millions of men, women and children. Officially one in sixteen inhabitants of London is not British. The actual figure is probably higher. New York is much the same. So are Toronto, Paris, Berlin, Sydney, Capetown. In every major town and city a percentage of the population is immigrant. Yet the story of what it's all about has never been told by those who are most intimate with it—the women who make immigration possible. During the upheaval, women double their responsibilities, to keep the family together physically and emotionally, to ease the disruption of their lives in the place where they settle.

Though it can be useful to be interviewed and studied by the 'experts', there is nothing more useful than speaking for ourselves. No matter what anyone else has said, there is always more to be said until women have spoken. In this case, nothing else can more effectively dispel the suspicion and ignorance with which immigrants are viewed. Once these experiences are brought to public attention, the debate on immigration can never be the same.

This book enables Black, immigrant women to give

their stories and perceptions in their own words. The Wages for Housework Campaign used our Women's Centre to hold the public meeting where Margaret Prescod-Roberts spoke in 1977. Norma Steele's speech was given in Paris at a Black women's conference the same year. The speeches bring into dazzling focus the reality that has been so distorted to the detriment of immigrant and non-immigrant.

All of us present at the meeting with Margaret Prescod-Roberts heard her with profound relief. Each of us felt she was speaking to our own experience. Although the hard truth was more startling than any provocative newspaper headline, the effect was to bring women into a much deeper understanding of how much our lives are dictated by the same needs, concerns and hopes regardless of more apparent differences. Those of us who were not immigrant saw the close similarities with our own experience. Some of us had been born in England but spent our childhood abroad before returning as 'foreigners'. Many remembered the move from countryside to town, from town to city. Many rediscovered that we or our parents were immigrant and, Black or white, we recalled the pain and anger we had repressed for years so that we could adapt and be acceptable.

Although these experiences had shaped our lives, the cost to ourselves had always been hidden and undervalued. The public fight over immigration focuses on how much we are given—housing, jobs, social security or the boat fare. We have never heard about how much we had to pay to immigrate and to stay in a second, third or maybe fourth country. Immigrant women pay not only in terms of money but also heartbreak. As housewives it has always meant more housework—reorganising and reuniting the family, easing the emotional trauma. The speeches describe in graphic detail how every penny was saved, the tears that were or were not cried, how much had to be learnt. Then we can see that housewives have made the major contribution to integration with the native community and to community relations. Once this work and pain is highlighted, we also see that we are owed far more than we owe.

Since these speeches were made, payment for housework, wages for motherhood, financial independence, home responsibility payments have become widely debated all over the world. An indication of that is the Welfare resolution passed in the U.S. at the historic International Women's Year Conference in Houston, Texas, in November 1977, attended by 20,000 women. For immigrant women who are the poorest and the most hardworking, this represents a major step forward in their struggle against poverty and dependence, and to win their due. We have included that resolution as a suitable ending for this book.

We are publishing this book as a contribution to the information on which decisions are made about women and about immigration. For in this kind of dialogue between housewives meeting as mothers, wives, grandmothers, sisters, daughters—immigrant and non-immigrant, Black and white—the fundamental information emerges, information that no statistics can prove or disprove. It is information that cannot be ignored.

Solveig Francis
Housewives in Dialogue
P.O. Box 287
London NW6 5QU
England

We are grateful to the Gulbenkian Foundation which helped to make this publication possible.

WE'RE IN BRITAIN FOR THE MONEY

NORMA STEELE

I came to England from Jamaica in 1962, a year after my parents. Why did my parents send for me? So I could escape the drudgery and the kind of housework mapped out for West Indian women, escape the poverty mapped out for Black women. That is, to be brought up in a house and a society where we thought there would be less physical work, to be able to get the kind of education which gives access to a better job—a job with more pay and less work.

I can tell you, and any other Jamaican woman can tell you, that housework in Jamaica is really tough, whether you live in the town or in the country. I have lived in both the town (with my parents) and in the country (with my grandparents). In the country, there are very few rented houses and plenty of work—hard unpaid work. People have to build their own homes from the cheapest material available, cheap timber. Cheap in the short run that is, because it's expensive to keep up. There are not many homes with electricity and running water, so cooking is done on kerosene stoves or over open fires in an outhouse. (The smoke from the fire

8

would be too much in the house.) Water has to be carried from a spring and could be some miles away. Firewood has to be gathered. Inside the house, all work has to be done without the aid of machines. Shopping has to be done every day as nothing stays fresh for long in the summer months—not even in an icebox, and of course ice is expensive, and there is little chance of getting any if you live far from the main roads. But at least there's plenty of space for the kids to play and you don't have to watch them all the time.

In the town, there's a desperate shortage of houses, and rents are very high. You have four or five separate one-storey houses with a courtyard in the middle. We just call it a yard as although all kinds of activities go on there—from raising chickens to washing clothes at the communal standpipe—certainly it's no place for courting. Each house usually contains four rooms, each occupied by separate families who share a communal kitchen and shower rooms. All the children share playing in the dusty yard. Can you imagine, the noise from the children, the fighting, the stench from the chicken coops and goat droppings? All the emotional housework of trying to keep sane and keep the children safe, and worrying about them while working on a second job. Because you take on a paid job to maintain yourself and the children as there are hardly any State benefits.

Paid jobs are mainly limited to domestic work—going to clean other people's houses, washing their clothes, cooking for them, waiting on them—and all you get in return is a pittance. All that housework and then home again, to start all over again doing physical and emotional housework. And the mothers ask, 'Is there no end to this struggle, this vicious circle of housework, housework? Life must be easier abroad.'

So you work harder to save up the fare, taking on a third and even fourth job, and the children work harder to get good grades in school and to learn to speak

English or French 'correctly'—and also take on paid jobs to help themselves and their mothers. Because they all feel and know that things will be better soon—as soon as they get to England. Everybody thinks so because all the white people they know not only say England is better but they all have big houses, big cars, fine clothes and lots of money. Your mother is even working for a white family that pays more than the Black families, and they have a washing machine and a vacuum cleaner. As part of the upheaval, as children we accept we will have to stay with Grannie or an aunt in the country for a while until our mother saves up and sends for us. In the meantime at least we will get parcels of clothes with money for school fees and food.

But when I arrived in the great metropolis, my school grades weren't good enough—although the exams had been based on the British exams. My mother was still forced to go out to work, but even worse, she wound up doing night shift work—working as a nurse in a hospital. We had to share a house with other people. Other Black and white people. The women, including the white women (some of whom were also from different countries), were working as cleaners, nurses—doing low paid dirty jobs in the service industries. Having to do housework in the mornings and the rest in the evenings. And this was really hard as the house was damp and cold and no matter how much cleaning and polishing you did, it still looked grubby and smelt dank. The women also had to cook and clean for their men and for the single men too, as this was easier than having to clean up after them as they weren't used to housework. My mother, though, would tell me not to do anything for the men. They assumed that because I was a girl I should be doing housework. But my mother told me she didn't bring me here for that. She had to put up with cleaning up after the patients and with cleaning the house and she was determined I shouldn't have to do the same. She had to do all this for us, and also she had to help the rest of the family here and in Jamaica. So I was to make sure I worked hard at school and got on.

My mother had to really struggle on that one wage to look after us here and send money home. My parents were divorced shortly after coming here and at first she had fought hard to get some money from my father. But then she decided she wouldn't bother, as each time he came round he wanted something in return and she wasn't going to have that. She wanted the money but she didn't want any more work, which is what it would mean each time my father came round. Scenes of quarelling, big trauma and temper tantrums were not unusual.

She already had enough coping with me, as while I was the good girl at school, at home it was another matter. I would cuss my mother, tell her she didn't speak well, how I hated Jamaican food, and complain she never turned up at parent-teacher meetings. Whenever I look back I remember how I treated her all those years, and the pain and grief I must have caused her. And I see all the housework she still has to do, that my grandmother does, that my great-grandmother had done, my aunts and cousins—and all that work for free. All that slave labour without a wage, without being paid. And here I see all the wealth in England and in Paris and in New York that was created and continues to be created by our labour and we are still so poor.

White women are also poor, and this is what Black women have seen by immigrating to England. White women are also forced to do unpaid housework and are also forced to take on low-paid second jobs. And when you look at the wealth in London and look at the ordinary women (which are the great majority) you can see they are not getting the wealth of these countries. Women's lack of money is international. As women we

11

produce workers for the wars, we produce workers for the factories, the mines—for all the dangerous but profit-making industries of the world. For without our well cared for, able-bodied children—the past and future workers of society—there wouldn't be a British Empire or French Empire or Dutch Empire or whatever Empire, and there wouldn't be these multi-corporations.

So when Black women come to Britain, the U.S. or any other metropolitan countries—the countries where the money is—we are here, there, for the money, not the weather. And when our children refuse to take on low-paid dirty jobs, when mothers refuse to work at home without being paid, when women refuse to take second jobs with long hours, poor equipment, dirty work—it is out of struggles that have gone on for hundreds of years that we are refusing to continue working for free or for a pittance.

BRINGING IT ALL BACK HOME

MARGARET PRESCOD-ROBERTS

I'm going to talk about being here for the money—in England and also in the United States which is where I'm living right now—and it's important to start by talking about where that money came from in the first place.

I think it's very clear to us now that huge British fortunes and American fortunes were made off our backs from as far back as slavery. Usually when we think about slavery the image we get is of the cotton fields, the sugar cane fields and all that kind of work. But it's also very clear that the key property the owner had was the slaves themselves, and women played a crucial part in producing that property, in producing those slaves, in raising and looking after everyone, including each other. Black women were also crucial in raising and looking after the master and his family.

In talking about slavery, then, what's usually left out or barely mentioned is the housework, the pivotal importance of housework, the huge amount of house-work that went on, whether it was in the slave master's house or in the hovels where most slaves lived. And

13

emerging out of the housework of slavery, the housework that Black women were doing inside and outside the house of the master, is the figure of the mammy, the Black mammy, which is a figure we're all familiar with. In the United States you see it all the time on Aunt Jemima pancake boxes, and practically everyone in the U.S. recognises that figure, with her head wrapped in a kerchief, as the Black mammy. And we can see that internationally; the Black mammy figure has become a personification of all the housework, the labour, that Black women had to do in those days of slavery and continued to do after the abolition of slavery.

What did the work of the mammy involve? It involved reproducing everyone, and by that I mean not just bearing children but raising them, looking after the men, other women, yourself, making sure everyone was fit for the next day. And reproducing not only her own children, her man and herself, but also reproducing the master and his family, his children, his wife. The mammy was responsible for keeping everyone going.

As part of that, in the time of slavery and also later, the Black woman was responsible for satisfying the master sexually. Clearly that was part of the work of being a mammy. When we saw the master choosing our daughter to come and work in the Great House, we knew very well that a big part of that work would be doing sexual work for him, and some of our children had to begin that work at a very early age. It was very clear that sexually serving the master was part of the job. You slept with the master, you did the cooking and cleaning, and you looked after the mistress, doing physical and emotional housework for her. Quite often you had to advise her on how to deal with her problems, how to deal with problems with her children, her inlaws, how to get her man interested in her and all that kind of thing. We hear about it in stories from the time of slavery, we see it in the movies, we read

14

about it in books, we saw it in *Gone with the Wind*—always the Black mammy taking on the responsibility of reproducing the white mistress in the house. And also looking after the children from when they were babies. Often it was the mammy who fed the children from her own breast, who really did most of the work of raising those white children.

MAMMY AS PROTAGONIST
But during that period we really see two things happening in the master/Black woman slave relationship. On the one hand, we see the way in which the master extracted work from all of us, but on the other hand we also see Black women using that role of mammy, and the power that she was able to build up in that role, to make a struggle against that master/slave relationship.

Many of the stories that we don't hear much of are about the mammies who would slip poison in the food of the masters, the mammy providing hiding places for runaways, stories of making a struggle within the master's house itself, which is part of what being a 'house nigger' was. Being a 'house nigger' meant having some access to food that the other slaves didn't have, or some item of clothing that the other slaves didn't have, and in some way getting some wages. The mammy was in a position to *take* some wages, whether it was wages in the form of food or articles of clothing, or maybe a few books that you stole from the master's library so that you and others had a chance to learn how to read. So in that situation, the mammy became a very central figure in the kind of organisation that went on against slavery, and was a point of reference in making a struggle to win wages, to take back some of the master's wealth.

The women were also using the power of raising the white children, and advising the white women, to pass on a lot of what is our culture. It's no accident that

15

in the United States today we can see and feel the influence of Black culture on white Americans. That process didn't happen accidentally. That process began with what was passed from the mammy to the children of the master who were her responsibility, her charge. (This process also continued after slavery.) So that we can see within the housework of the Black woman in the time of slavery two things were going on: the utilisation of that woman to reproduce the master and his family, and at the same time that woman making a struggle against that work, to destroy that work.

THE WEST INDIES AFTER SLAVERY

The image of the Black mammy didn't end with emancipation, and again that's no accident. We don't have a figure of a Black pappy, if you know what I mean, but of the Black mammy, and there's a very good reason for that—because she was a slave and she's also a woman. Slavery ended, because Black people won some cash wages (not much). But women were still expected to do most housework unpaid, so the role of the mammy continued to a degree. I'll talk specifically about the West Indian situation, where after emancipation many of the families lived around the tenantry, which is the living area for the workers around the plantation house. Life in the tenantry, as we can well imagine, was extremely difficult. Black women continued to work as labourers in the field. But the relationship of the mammy also continued, with Black women often working as maids in the plantation house and again having to provide sexual favours, whether they were working in the master's house or just living in the tenantry. And the struggle continued, too, in the way Black women were again using this relationship, using this situation, to get as much as possible for themselves and their families.

I remember, for example, in the village in Barbados

16

where I grew up, women being very careful about picking the father of their child. It was no accident that a plantation owner or an overseer may have ten, fifteen or twenty children spread around in the tenantry. We know how many of these women were raped and were therefore forced to be pregnant. But many women also decided to have the owner or overseer as the father of their child because having this man to father their child meant getting some access to some wages for themselves and security for the child. At least they could go to this man for money to get a pair of shoes for the child, get some money for books for school, get some new clothing; it was his child too, after all. It wasn't much, but again it was a way of getting some wages, so quite often you found those fathers being very carefully chosen.

Another aspect of picking a father was colour, which is something we don't like to talk about much, who's light skinned and who's darker, and the relation of this to wages. In the choice of the father the mother sometimes calculated that a child who's a bit lighter skinned will have a better chance in this world, things will be easier for that child. These women were not fools. When you're functioning in a situation of scarcity and you have to worry every day about how your children are going to eat, and how you are going to eat, you think about these things. And you organise your life in such a way as to make sure you get the money you must have, to make sure you get what you and your children need to survive.

So again we see that mammy relationship continuing with the emancipation, and again used by the mammy, but in a slightly different way than during the time of slavery. But it still means housework, the work of reproducing ourselves, reproducing our children, reproducing the men that we're dependent on because we're getting some kind of wage from them in some kind of

17

way. You know, sometimes it was just the prestige of having Mr. So-and-so as your child's father, which didn't mean necessarily getting the cash in your hand, but you knew that when you went down to the school or when you went down to the officials, they could take a look at your child and you could say, 'Well, Mr. So-and-so is his father,' and right away that child would have access to something. It was either cash, or services, or things that money can buy—but one way or another getting some kind of wage.

I've been talking about the mammy and about her work, that housework, because it has everything to do with the way capital—meaning big British and American money—was able to accumulate the vast amount of wealth and fortune that it did. It's important to talk about that, and it's specially important for us as Black women to talk about that when we say we're here for the money, because what we're saying is that we helped to create that wealth, that we were *pivotal* in creating that wealth. Don't tell us that we have to stay in the West Indies, that we have to work three times as hard to create new wealth for the West Indies. Because we have done three hundred years or more of labour— labour that I have done, my mother, my grandmother and people before me have done. When we look around, when I looked around my village, when I looked around Barbados, the wealth wasn't there. It was some place else. It was in London, it was in New York, from the French-speaking West Indies it was in Paris, from the Dutch-speaking West Indies it was in Amsterdam.

We can see, then, what was behind the kind of organisation that went on within the village to make sure that at least we got somebody to go away, to emigrate, to where our own wealth was.

HAVING FAMILY AWAY
There was a very high level of organisation to get the

18

money or the means together to make sure you had some member of your family going to either the U.S., Canada or Britain. What was that about? It was because, looking around us, we knew that our lives in the village were about work, were about years, centuries of hard work. Every year, day in day out, it's the same thing. And it was clear that the wealth that we were creating was not there—we had to go and get it. So having family away, and by away I mean abroad, in North America or in Europe, meant immediately the possibility of getting some money. I remember in Barbados there being some jokes about it, because quite often when somebody had family away, or if somebody left to go to London or New York, some folks immediately began to put on what you call 'airs'; you know, they started acting a little different, a little bit more powerful. Everybody used to say, 'You know, So-and-so think he great 'cause he got family in America' (or London or Paris, etc.). But there was a very material base to that, because immediately having somebody away meant the possibility of some money. You knew that shortly you could expect some letter with maybe a little $5, a little $10, a little $20 that was crucial to your survival and the survival of the immediate family.

So family abroad meant the possibility of access to a wage, getting some kind of money, and also the things money can buy. Those of us here who are poor immigrants, specifically from the West Indies, may remember the parcels that came from abroad, maybe once a year, and if your family away was doing pretty good maybe twice a year. You really looked forward to that because you knew you were going to get some new dress, a new pair of shoes that may not fit but you stuff your feet into them anyway, some canned goods that half the time you may not necessarily know how to prepare. I remember the first time I ate 'cream style corn'. I just opened the can and ate the thing and it was disgusting.

19

(You were supposed to heat it.) I couldn't understand why these Americans ate that stuff. Sometimes you'd get a ham, and if you were lucky the ham got to you before it began to rot—at Christmas your box may show up with a rotten ham. But all the things in that box were very important to us, crucial to us.

Paying school fees, for example. When time came for the new school term, you were nervous. Every day you see the postman, you ask, 'Letter from America?' Because you knew that the little $20 in that letter was going to make the difference to whether your children were going to go to school, to whether they were going to get some shoes on their feet or not. So this whole struggle to get people abroad, to go away, was a move to take back the wealth that we have created, something that is ours. This is clearly the way *we* have used immigration.

THE STATE'S PLAN FOR IMMIGRATION

It's also clear that the State has a plan for immigration. We see a situation where workers in one place refuse to do some jobs, say: 'We're not going to do this stuff any more, we want some more money, we want some higher wages, we're tired of these long hours, we're not going to do that any more.' The State can then go and find some wageless people somewhere else. In the case of England, it was the West Indies, India, Pakistan, Southern Europe, etc. They bring in workers from the Third World to do that job at a lower wage than the workers who are living here, immediately creating a division between the different workers. Because the people already here are going to say, 'What is this? I'm making a struggle against this work, demanding higher wages, and these people are going to come in and do the same work for less money?' Clearly we can see the way the State set up the use of immigration to really undermine the struggles of workers, the struggles that workers were making.

On the one hand, we can see the State's plan for immigration, but also we've always had our own plan for immigration. And that's part of what this meeting tonight is about, about taking back what's ours and about refusing those divisions, and refusing the way the State attempts to undermine us. And we're saying, 'We want the money, and we know some other folks who want the money, and we're going to come together, and together we're going to take the money. How about that?'

GETTING MONEY AT HOME

But before saying a little bit more about that, I'd like to say more about this whole question of housework, and destroying the image of the mammy, to say more about the struggle for the wage as I saw it in the village where I grew up in Barbados. I've already talked about the connection between picking a particular father for your children and getting money, those sexual relations that went on to do with getting money. But something else not talked about much is the high level of prostitution that went on in the villages and in the towns. In the villages it would be picking up men who had a little bit of a wage, the plantation man, the overseer, some man who had a job in town, meaning he had a wage coming in. I remember how we always knew in the village when the sail boats and big ships came to Bridgetown, the capital, because that meant there was the possibility for somebody's child to be making some money. And quiet as it's kept, word was passed within families. Information about 'Well, the sailors—well, you know, the boats are here . . .' Mothers, grandmothers, aunts and cousins busily prepared by making a new dress for relations going to Bridgetown. In other words, whole families were supported off the money that women made from prostitution, children were raised on it,

21

sometimes whole families, including the extended families, were supported on it. So prostitution was another means of getting some wages for us in that situation.

Then there's the use of the Church, which I should say something about. I mean, being from Barbados which is 'Little England'. It's clear that the State used the Church of England, that it was part of the way we were ruled. The island itself is divided into eleven parishes. Each parish has a parish church, the big main church. And many people in the parish went to Church. There's a lot of talk among some young people these days about 'these foolish women in the Church'. But it was clear what the women were doing. The Church meant religion. The Church meant a social occasion. The Church meant getting together with people like yourself. And the Church also meant getting access to a number of things besides that. Sometimes it was direct cash, not much usually, from the 'poor box'. You go in with your story and you get a little bit of money. But also in terms of finding a job, your chances were better if you got in good with the rector or the priest of the parish church. As a little girl I always used to wonder about that, about the women who got in good with the priest, because after all the priest is supposed to be married to God after his wife and what not, but still there were some women who were pretty friendly with the priest. And when your child got into some trouble, your teenage boy out liming all day—hanging around a shady area, or a shop, etc., exchanging remarks with other boys and with passers-by—when your boy won't find a job, you have to feed him, what are you going to do? You go to the priest who has some kind of in with some bureaucrats, with somebody in town whom you don't have any access to, and that's a way again of you seeking out the wage, of using the priest and using the Church in that particular way.

So the struggle that we were all making for that

22

money didn't begin when we got here, when we got to New York or when we got to London. It started in the villages and in the towns that we were from in the West Indies, because we needed that money to survive. In other words, the struggle for that money and also to destroy that work—that mammy image—is nothing new.

LEAVING HOME

Part of the organising, the preparation to go away, was exchanging stories about what life was like in England and in America. What were the accents, the way people walked and the way people talked and all that kind of thing. But very key in the preparation was a realisation that there was some rise in the level of power; that when you go to London and you go to New York, you don't have to be shuffling and you don't have to be grovelling; you can lift your head upright and do what it is you have to do and demand your money. And a perfect example of that would be the struggle of West Indian nurses in London and New York. I mean they don't always fit the figure of the kind mammy who gives—pardon the expression—a titty to everybody, if you know what I mean: comforting everybody and being so nice. In New York, some folks say, 'Man, you get one of those West Indian nurses, hell, they don't wanna do *nothing.*' There's a grain of truth in that. You figure I'm a nurse here in London or in New York or in Toronto, 'I'm going to demand my money, and *don't* expect me to be nice or smile just because I'm Black, because I'm not going to do it.' So again it was clear that coming over to the States or England, and the level of power that you then had to enable you to struggle for the money, was a very key part of destroying that mammy image. Because that Black nurse, she don't fit no mammy image nowhere.

We can see, then, the struggle for the money at home, what family abroad in the metropolitan areas meant, and what was the organising within the village to go abroad. It was a big thing.

I remember in my family it was a very big thing. Everybody would sit around and talk serious—I mean, I was young and I was scared because they'd be sitting around talking, making plans to go, and I knew that some stuff was going to come down, some big split. I was going to be split off from my friends, from the way of life that I knew. So first there was all of the emotional housework that we had to do for each other in preparing to go. And the mother explains to the children, it's going to be a better life, and all these stories circulate about how the streets are paved with gold, all those kind of lies; you know, you've heard them: 'In New York City the streets are paved with gold' and 'In London there's all this money' and all that kind of thing. I mean, I believe some of those lies were told really as part of holding ourselves together. It's very difficult to leave a place like the West Indies. I mean, to say 'We didn't come for the weather' is more than the truth. It's very difficult to leave the weather, the mangoes, the sea, and all of that to come up here, and it really took a lot of emotional housework just keeping ourselves together to go.

I remember my father putting up the 'For Sale' sign outside the house, a typical little Barbados wooden house. He and my mother had struggled for years to build that house and to pay for that house. And I remember the morning he painted the sign and was ready to put that sign up. He just sat in a chair, long drops of water coming out of his eyes, coming down his face. I felt all of that, I felt that somehow I had to comfort my father and say, you know, 'It'll be all right, it really won't be too bad.' My mother also had that emotional housework. So when I talk about the emotional housework of just preparing to leave, that's serious. That's the uprooting of everything you've ever known, to go someplace else, not really knowing what's ahead of you, what's before you. And that's a lot of hard work.

Then saying goodbye to friends and relatives. Many of us remember seeing them, driving down the road to the airport, and neighbours—people that you've known all your life—just standing by the side of the road, waving, telling you to remember them. And you knew that was also mixed, when they said, 'Remember me when you get to America. You're not going to forget me, you hear.' Because you knew that meant two things: 'Remember that we still have between us all the things we've shared,' but also the other side of that was 'When you get to that money, remember me, 'cause I'm still here.' So there was always a double edge going on, and you could feel that double edge, and that's a lot of work. You know, it takes a lot to deal with that.

There was also arranging for childcare, a very big thing if it was the mother who was going.

Getting together in a family and deciding who would go, the lucky ones were the families where the women went. And the reason for that was that you knew very well that the women were going to be sending back the money, particularly if they left a few children or they had a mother or a grandmother back home. Quite often the men would come over, maybe leave a family in Barbados, but pick up with another woman in London or New York to reproduce them and do the house-work—and start another family. So when the men went by themselves, you were taking a chance because you didn't know what you were going to get. Your best bet was to get a woman to go because you knew that a woman was tied to her housework, the housework of reproducing her kids back home or her mother or her grandmother or somebody in the family. Tied to that housework and feeling identified with it, and feeling

25

responsible to the point that she got up off of that $30 and sent it back. The man, it was a different story, it was a different question. Sometimes in the village there would be occasions when Mr. So-and-so would come back from England and he would bring his new wife and child. But meanwhile Mr. So-and-so had a woman and two children up the road. That was quite common.

To get back to the preparation for going and what to do about the children. Particularly in the case of the woman, you often had to leave your children behind. You just couldn't take everybody. My mother came with all three of us and I remember she and my father went through hell to raise the money for all of us to come. Often you just didn't have the money to bring the children, or because of the problems you were having with immigration and your visa and that kind of nonsense you couldn't bring them anyway. So you would have to figure out who would care for your children when you were away. Organising that was part of the housework of preparing to go, a very big part of it. And then there was the separation itself from the children.

MOVING UP
In New York and I suppose it happens here as well, some West Indians are labelled 'upwardly mobile'. The ones that come here, work hard at a job, do all kinds of overtime to move up in this world, buy a house, eventually buy a car and all that kind of thing. I know among a younger crowd sometimes there's contempt for those West Indians. 'They don't know nothing, they ain't making no kind of struggle, all they here for, all they after is the money, getting on.' My grandmother was one of those 'upwardly mobile' West Indians. She used to work cleaning people's houses, and during the war she worked in a factory. She saved

her money. She learned how to sew so she could make every piece of clothes, so she didn't have to go into the store and buy anything, because she knew she had a daughter with children back home. It was her that was sending those parcels and she had to have the money to do that. And also there was her dream that some day her daughter and her grandchildren would be able to come, and she had to provide for them.

So I can't look down on my grandmother and the struggle that she made to get that money, to be 'upwardly mobile', because she was making a way for us. It was because of the struggle that she made that I am here now saying openly, 'I'm here for the money. I want my money.' My grandmother may not have been able to say it in that way. But it was clear that the struggle that she made, made it possible for me to be here making the struggle I'm making. I'm not saying that there isn't anything to learn in terms of this upwardly mobile business. I'll say more about that later. But clearly when you have the kind of dependency of children and family and people you know back home scraping for every penny to survive, that means a lot of work, always trying to accumulate something, get some security, some stability. That really ties you to that paid job and forces you to accept any job because you know that you can't do without it. But it also makes it possible for your children and your grandchildren—like me—to come around and say, 'I refuse it. I ain't going to do it no more.'

BEING AN IMMIGRANT

So there's the housework before you get here; then when you arrive having to deal with getting a job, all that kind of thing; and then just the housework of being an immigrant, having to put up with all the names and stuff they call you. I remember in high school in New York I had a teacher who in front of the class used to call me 'swamp woman' because I was from the West Indies. That was supposed to be a big joke. But I didn't think it was so funny. People saying you live in shacks, you live in huts back there, or calling you 'coconut heads' and 'monkey chasers'. Which were some of the familiar terms in New York. That's a lot of housework, coming home after a day of that kind of harassment and knowing that you had to get yourself together to go out the next day and deal with that stuff all over again. That's a lot of housework

And then there was the pressure on the mother because it was her that had to be patching you up, and telling you, 'It's OK, it's not too bad, and some day you're going to go back home anyway.' Which is always the big dream. 'Some day we're going back home, so don't worry about it, this is just a little while that we have to put up with this.'

There was that housework, then, of reproducing ourselves, reproducing our children, learning the new ways, the new machinery. Discovering the big lie about the modern kitchen that we're going to get, that's going to cut down on our housework, right? Big joke! There's having to learn how to use all these new machines that they tell us really will give us more time, more leisure time and all that kind of thing. We know a lot better now.

Even childcare in a metropolitan area is a big problem. If you live in a village in an extended family, you know that if your child's outside somewhere, someone will be looking out for her. If your child is out in the street and your neighbour down the road sees your child in some mess, that woman is going to take the responsibility of dealing with that child. But in Brooklyn, or in London, you're stuck in that apartment. You're there with that kid, you can't expect that child to be out on the street and be taken care of. You know the day care situation is lousy, you're not in that extended family, so you have a big problem on your hands. So when they talk about the reduction of housework, we know by now that that's a lie.

Also speaking from a West Indian experience (but I think it happens with other immigrants, too), another part of the work of being an immigrant is being expected to be two people at once. You have to try to maintain two 'cultures'. You've come from a situation where you're used to doing things in one way, and you're told, well there's something a little bit wrong with that, you have to adjust it a little bit. Then you're going to have some people that tell you, 'You're sounding very American now, what happened?' or 'You've been here for five years and you sound like you just got off the boat, what happened?' So I mean, either way, you're damned if you do, damned if you don't. You're stuck with some people telling you you should keep all of your West Indian ways, and others saying, 'What's the matter with you? You don't seem interested in mixing.' Juggling those is housework too!

This kind of adjusting is something I had to deal with all through high school. I remember my sister and me going home from school and practising saying 'Yeah', and how to chew gum the right way. We did these things because we were catching hell at school and with our friends, and we knew that this kind of practising was one way of surviving. But it was a very schizophrenic state because we liked the way we were at home and we didn't think there was anything wrong with us.

BLACK WOMEN IN THE SIXTIES

Now before talking about organising for the money where we are at this particular point, I think it's important to say a bit about the struggles that went on in the United States in the sixties—the Black Movement— because that had a very big impact internationally.

What's quite often left out in describing the sixties is the part played by Black women and the struggles Black women led around welfare. Demanding welfare money directly from the government for housework, demanding money for ourselves and for our children.

In the sixties Black women took to the streets, taking over welfare offices, leaving their children down at the welfare offices, destroying files and saying to the U.S. government, 'Look, we're tired, we've had enough, we're tired of all this work—we *over*work. You owe us something, there's some wages due here.' We saw the welfare rolls—the number of people claiming welfare—not only doubling but just about quadrupling, with many Black folks moving from the South of the U.S.A. into northern urban areas where the payments were higher, getting on to welfare rolls, demanding their money.

I don't think it's an accident that, at the same time that Black women, primarily Afro-American Black women, were leading a struggle to demand money directly from the government, in the West Indian community the women were making a struggle around the schools. We want education for our children. 'Learn the book' was something that we always heard at home. (Barbados has the highest rate of literacy in the world.) I don't think West Indian women have any illusions about education. Every day inside and outside the schools we have to struggle with people telling us that things we knew to be right growing up in the West Indies are wrong, and that we have to adopt some other kind of way. So we knew what was going on in the schools. Every mother knew what education meant and about how it was turning her child against her, creating another division. But it was clear that learning the book and getting that piece of paper—a diploma or a degree—meant getting access to some kind of wage where maybe your child didn't have to be a street

30

sweeper, or didn't have to go round cleaning white people's houses, but got access to some kind of decent job. Black American women were also very much involved in the struggle around education, and a very interesting coming together happened. I'll give an example of that in the City University of New York.

Back in the sixties in the struggle around education we were saying, 'Look, you've got to open up the doors of these universities to Black people, we don't like this stuff any more, all this business about us being kept out: you better let us in.' It was a hell of a struggle. Finally, the City University said any graduate from a New York City high school would be eligible to enter the University without needing all of the various qualifications. In other words, open admissions. But the women in the Black community were saying, 'Look, that's not enough. Fine, you tell us we can come, but how are we going to get there? How are we going to buy our books? What are we going to put on our backs? It was clear that open admissions were useless unless we won some money. Which is exactly what happened in 1966 in New York City.

In the City University something called the Seek Programme was established. Search for Education, Elevation and Knowledge. The Seek Programme was a programme largely for poor students and minorities. The vast majority of them were women, including women on welfare. And the men were mostly the sons of women on welfare. Beginning in 1966, every few weeks these students would receive some wages, a stipend, what is called in Britain a maintenance grant, for going to school. 'Just for going to school.' But that's another full-time job, and we'd won payment for it. So we can see a coming together, the struggle for welfare and the struggle around education in getting programmes like Seek, a coming together for that money directly from the government. Within the Seek

31

Programme today there are large numbers of immigrant students—Latin Americans, Haitians, West Indians—immigrant students in the University collecting their wages.

GETTING TOGETHER

We see the coming together of all those struggles of immigrant and Black American students, getting together to build a mobilisation to stop the cutbacks, and Black Women for Wages for Housework helped make that happen.

When the crisis first hit New York City, one of the first things they said would go is the Seek Programme, which was 57 per cent women. Also there were big headlines in the newspapers about welfare fraud going on in the City University, students collecting welfare, and also collecting a stipend—the maintenance grant—from the University.* That's supposed to be fraud, but we knew very well that the two of them together weren't enough to make it, weren't enough to live on. So we found a situation where action had to be taken, and the first move was the women on the campus took their autonomy from men.

The women said, 'Look, they're talking about welfare fraud, and when they talk about welfare that's 90 per cent women,† that's us. We're in this situation, we have to move, because if we're out of this college, we're back out on the street, or we're back home without a penny.' And *nobody* is interested in going back into their homes without a penny. Nobody wants to do that

---

*Students collect money from the University in three forms:
a) a stipend or maintenance grant
b) book money—a grant towards the cost of books
c) tuition money—a grant towards the cost of tuition fees.
Many Seek students get all three of these, and some of these students also collect welfare.

† Ninety per cent of all welfare recipients in the U.S. are women.

too much these days. So we find, then, these women using the International Wages for Housework Campaign as a point of power because—drawing on the experience of Black women and on the struggles that Black women had made for that money directly from the government—the Campaign was saying, first of all, the rest of us who are in these marriages, we're sick of this dependent situation; that's ruining the relationship with the men. I mean, it's intolerable. We don't want this dependency any more.

Second of all, what about the work that we're *all* doing in our homes? What makes the work of a housewife with two children in the suburbs respectable and that of a woman on welfare degrading? Does getting the welfare cheque mean you're not a housewife? Does going to school mean you're not a housewife? Living in any neighbourhood (except the very rich, I don't know about them) *is a lot of housework for women.* Some women maybe live out in the suburbs and have a house with a little white fence around and all that stuff. And the Black woman is in another neighbourhood where she has to do some other kinds of housework: it's a lot of work fighting rats and roaches and that kind of thing; worrying about your kids being mugged, you being mugged, and maybe it's your kid who's doing the mugging because he doesn't have any money—and you sure don't have any to give him. But in both situations you're doing housework and making a fight to demand that money directly from the government, which is a huge power, especially for those Black women who were making that struggle in the sixties around welfare but were feeling the isolation from other women.

Now when the State decides that it's going to move against women on welfare, it can no longer isolate those women and say, 'They're just some Black women over there who are lazy, who want to collect some money,' because there's a whole international campaign

33

going on with women saying, 'No more. We're all doing housework and we're all going to get together and demand our money.'

So the Queen's College Women's Action Group, made up of Seek students, teachers and other staff, began to say: 'We're not going back into that home penniless, and as a matter of fact we're doing *two* full-time jobs if we're a woman and we're a student. One is housework, the other is schoolwork, and we're going to expose both of them. And we already know that women internationally are making this case and demanding that money, so you can't isolate us any more.' The other thing we're saying is, 'Look, this whole campus/community split that's going on with us and the rest of the women out there is absurd, because that's where we come from; you can't separate us off.'

The Action Group women, together with other women in the community and with Black Women for Wages for Housework (U.S.A.), made a mobilisation to demand an increase in the stipend money and a few other things—like free day care on campus for all of the women, not just the students but also the teachers and the cleaning staff and the typists; like increases in the money that's given out to pay for tuition; like increases in the money that's given out to pay for books; like an advocacy centre on campus where the women can come together and get information on housing, medicare, food stamps, and anything they're entitled to but don't know about or don't know how to get.

The way we organised made it possible for many of the immigrant women who were in the Seek Programme to come out and say, 'Look, I'm getting a pretty rotten deal here because when they look at my financial situation and the money that I'm making they don't include the money I have to send back home, and the fact that I may have a child back home that I have to support, or I may have a mother back there that I have to send money to; they don't take that into account when the college decides how much money it's going to give me on a student grant.' The Haitian women emerged and started talking a lot about what it was like for the women back in Haiti, and what it's like for Haitian women in New York.

The mobilisation made possible a coming together of a number of things. Those immigrant women were able to use that mobilisation as a point of power to talk about their situation and to participate openly within that struggle. And also the men who were Seek students who hadn't forgotten the experience of their mothers being on welfare, and so didn't feel threatened by women demanding money, but saw the advantage for them—the men were able to come around the Action Group and say, 'Well, we know there's something in here for us also, what can we do to help?' So the men worked on publicity. When we had confrontational meetings with the administration or various other 'officials', they would come along. They liked to function as security, you know, stand around and look tough and what not.

But what was clear within that mobilisation was that there was a whole different relationship between the men and the women from the relationship some of us had experienced in the male-dominated organisations of the sixties. An entirely different relationship where it was clear that the women were the point of reference. It was clear that when we women got together and talked about what *our* needs were and made a struggle around them, it was something that not only women were going to win by but all of us were going to win by. And those young bloods—the men—came right on time.

And there were some things that really puzzled a lot of the left and Black nationalists on campus, particularly those who had been toying with the idea of organising. They couldn't figure out why the men they

35

couldn't reach, whom they wrote off as unorganisable (or maybe just not worth it), the hustler types, men formerly from neighbourhood gangs, why these kinds of men were coming around the Action Group and saying, 'Hey, our slogan is "No Cuts Just Bucks",' which they got from the button of Black Women for Wages for Housework. They were walking around with the button on saying, 'No Cuts Just Bucks—right on!' They could definitely dig that.

The left and the nationalists couldn't understand what was going on with this women's group who were talking about the needs of all women and saying, 'We're not going to cut ourselves off from other women,' and getting all this support from these men. We talked about prostitution on and off the campus. A lot of prostitution that was happening on the campus—it's only begun to emerge. Some of it was connected to grades (a lot still needs to be uncovered about men teachers and their relationship to female students). Also some women were working on the game at weekends to make ends meet. We talked about lesbian women and about not being separated off from lesbian women. One thing that emerged was the paranoia about lesbian women at the women's centre on campus, and some women trying to keep the lesbian women out because they were worried that if somebody saw some lesbian women around the centre they would think that all of them were lesbian—and God forbid! We were told this by lesbian women who were stepping forward and saying, 'We're part of this, we want our money too, and we're going to be visible as lesbians in the fight for it.'

A lot of men were also threatening the women they knew, saying that if they came around the Women's Action Group they'd be labelled lesbian, to discourage 'their' women from participating. A lot of women were able to refuse this and say, 'You're not going to be able to use this bit about lesbianism as a threat.

Lesbians, so what? There are some lesbians around, you wanna meet some? You give me too much crap, and I know I have some other kind of option. So you're the one who'd better look out.' We really began to see, with the presence of that mobilisation and the power that came from the community and from an international campaign rooted in many communities, that a lot of women got the power to come out in a lot of ways.

And the other good news about the mobilisation is that we've won an increase in the cash. From this September, we won an increase in the book money. Victory is sweet. It's still not enough but it's in the right direction. All the bloods were going around saying, 'Yeah, No Cuts Just Bucks—right on!' You know, a lot more of them were smiling then. Also we're now negotiating with the administration about a day care centre on campus. Now everybody from the administration right down, practically every time they open their mouths, they feel they have to talk about the women on welfare; you know, 'We have to do something to help them,' using the kind of language that they didn't use before we came together. In a memo that we were able to hijack from the highest level of the University administration, we see them talking about the Seek Programme and other 'special programmes' being given priority, top priority. As a matter of fact they're even opening a new administrative line to pay somebody $43,000 a year, and the qualifications include having good relationships with community groups and knowing how to deal with student groups.

One of the high points of the mobilisation was a mass meeting of community people and students on campus with about 300 people present. We had the administration on the line. It was clear that, with the coming together of the campus and the community, and with immigrant students emerging in a way that they hadn't

37

before, we were able to win a lot of things and I'm sure we'll be feeling the impact of it all for some time.*

WE'RE HERE FOR THE MONEY

That mobilisation has been key in the coming together of the struggle around welfare and the struggle around education, and us saying openly as immigrants, 'Yes, we want the money, we're here for the money and we're no longer going to hide it, because we're involved in making a struggle for us to get the money and for others also to get that money.'

One thing that struck me when I first came to England is how poor most people are. I mean, I knew a lot of wealth has been stolen from Barbados and other colonies, but the British working class sure didn't get it. So when we're talking here about 'We've come for the money', what we have to keep in mind is exactly whose money it is. A lot of it is ours because we created it, but a lot of it also belongs to some other people. When we're making a struggle within an international campaign for wages for housework, we're saying we want

---

*We have won many victories since. The two most important to date are:

1) The President's Office at Queen's College set up a Child Care Committee, which has now submitted specific proposals for the funding of a day care centre with an opening date projected for the 1980/81 school year.

2) We have succeeded in winning a bill in the New York State Legislature, calling for an end to the deduction of tuition grant money from the welfare cheques of students on welfare. This would mean an increase of $750 to $900 in the cash available to welfare recipients who are students. We have managed to get support for this bill from the head of the Committee on Higher Education of the New York State Legislature, who is the sponsor of the bill and will introduce it on the floor of the Assembly. Support also comes from the Higher Education Representative in the Governor's Office and from the Office of the Commissioner of Social Services (Welfare) for New York State. (M.P.-R., August, 1979.)

that money internationally, for all of us. And we're precisely undermining the kinds of divisions that the Man—the State—has established and hopes to keep going, and undermining all of the fears that come with 'Well, if Black women say they want some money, that means they'll be taking something from some other poor slob out here,' from some other overworked working class person. So what's clear to us at this point is firstly the international is crucial for us, and secondly, we're making a struggle right where we are for that money, we're getting together with other women in making that struggle, so that together we can take it, take back what's ours.

This is the last round in destroying this mammy image, this mammy role, this mammy work. And something has become very clear to us. When we try to make an isolated struggle to destroy that image, which some upwardly mobile Blacks did—you know, 'I'm no longer on the same level as you, I'm now a social worker or a teacher, and I live in the suburbs and I now have a car,' etc.—they were always reminded somewhere along the line that they were a mammy just like anybody else. Because the rest of us Black women, the majority of us, are still at the bottom. Often we're told that we have an option, that if we don't want to be a mammy, we can be a 'lady'. But we've already learnt something from the white women who are now saying plenty about this 'lady' business. Not only that, but we've never forgotten what we knew about the ladies when we were cleaning their houses or in slavery. Because we were clearly identified as mammies, they were coming to us for advice about how to deal with their situation. And we saw how they were freaking out and quite often we had to hold them together. We learnt a lot about what this dependency on the men did to them. So we don't want that stuff either.

So we're rejecting the mammy image and rejecting

the lady image and the so-called mammies and ladies are coming together and demanding our money, taking our money. And that's what 'We're here for the money' and the International Wages for Housework Campaign is all about.

October 1977

WE COME
FROM ANOTHER FIELD

*I come from another field—the country of the slave.
If it is not a fit place for women, it is unfit for men
to be there.*

Sojourner Truth, 1867

The truth and clarity—the reality—of Margaret Prescod-Roberts' speech comes from organisation. It comes from organisation that begins by pooling and distilling the experience of our individual struggles into a common direction which is the common inheritance of the generations of struggle before us. It comes from organisation that begins with what our mothers taught us. It comes from organisation that begins with Black women.

COMING TO MEET THE MAN
At the bottom of the international hierarchy of work,* Third World women know best that we work in this hierarchy under the threat that the money we make will be taken by somebody else—when it every since already has: that we belong to this hierarchy because we do not belong to ourselves. For women hold up far more than

*Read Selma James, *Sex, Race and Class*, Bristol, Falling Wall Press, 1975.

41

half the sky—but we are not about to make a religion out of womanhood as a state of grace or style of work: there's a world of difference between working harder and being more powerful—and women, particularly Third World women, are tired of being blackmailed into identifying the two, making a virtue of our slavery.

We come from another field called home. We do housework there for no wages. The laundry and the cooking are not the half of it. We migrate every day—to school, to the welfare office, to second, third and fourth jobs, to other cities and countries—fixing our faces and clothes and hair to meet the Man.* We piece together children and men and other women for the same combat—to go and collect some wages to bring back home.

The movement of women of colour to get wages for the work we do can least afford to respect the national boundaries through which governments, business and industry have ripped us off. And the nationalism which makes a few men or women of colour the boss over the wealth that's left in the Third World costs us no less. The nationalism of Third World governments is the salvation of metropolitan government, business and industry: it veils our exploitation with a flag.

Metropolitan guilt about 'living off the Third World' is the other side of the coin of Third World nationalism: the Third World looks like another country outside the metropolis with no identity of interests and therefore no identity of struggle with more powerful sectors in the international hierarchy of work: the problem of how to take back the wealth for all the world's people is turned into an act of charity from the havelittles to the

*The Man—a unique Black American expression for the ultimate power of government, business and industry as well as the pecking order of mediators of that power: anyone acting as a boss or controller over other people's work, time and energy; in the way that the word is spoken, the tone of voice, it conveys the experience of both domination and resistance.

havenots.

GETTING IT TOGETHER
Immigration divides us every day: whether we are Blacks breaking into white jobs, women breaking into men's jobs, juniors breaking into seniors' jobs, suburbanites breaking into city jobs, or 'aliens' breaking into Americans' jobs. For that matter, Pan-Africanism might have been a great idea—but the waiting list of Black Americans and other Third World immigrants competing against each other for jobs at the phone company is something else.

In the United States, up through the 1950s, the history of slavery was considered no excuse for Black Americans not making it into the mainstream as white ethnic immigrants supposedly had. But in the 60s, beginning with women at home, at welfare offices, in the schools and on the streets, demanding money for food, clothing, housing and education for ourselves and our children, a massive movement of Black people claiming reparations from the Man for the unpaid work of centuries made a new yardstick of everyone's entitlement. So in the 70s white ethnics began to talk and organise much more about what they also have not: none of us immigrants have made it yet.

The delegation from the International Wages for Housework Campaign at the International Women's Year —National Women's Conference in November 1977 included Third World and white women who are Catholic, Protestant, Quaker, Jewish; Latin-American, African-American, West Indian, Native American, Ukrainian, Anglo-Saxon, Irish, Italian, Polish, German, Lithuanian, Austrian, Russian and Roumanian. Margaret Prescod-Roberts, a spokeswoman for the International Campaign, and a New York State delegate to the Conference, led the Wages for Housework contingent from among the delegates, while Wilmette Brown, co-founder

43

of Black Women for Wages for Housework (U.S.A.), led our lobbying from the floor. Together with other women from all races and regions, lesbian, prostitute, married and single, we won passage of the Women, Welfare, and Poverty resolution reprinted here.

The battle over welfare at Houston was for more money for the majority of women versus token positions for a few. Our fight for money of our own is not so we can join the Man in sitting on top of the world. Our victory is an open invitation to share the wealth.

Wilmette Brown
for Black Women for Wages for Housework (U.S.A.)
P.O. Box 830
Brooklyn, New York 11201
Tel: (212) 624-0847, (201) 923-9797

WOMEN,
WELFARE, AND POVERTY

The following resolution was passed at the International Women's Year—National Women's Conference held in Houston, Texas, 18-21 November, 1977, attended by 20,000 women. It replaced the 'official' resolution which had called for support for President Carter's welfare reform bill (H.R. 9030), then before Congress.

As well as throwing out the President's bill, its effects are still being felt in government policy and legislation. For example, Sarah Weddington, the President's special assistant on women's affairs, publicly stated in 1978 that the central issue for women is economic, and that the nub is payment to housewives.

Work to implement all the recommendations is continuing.

For those not familiar with the terms used, there is a note at the end explaining them.

The Federal and State governments should assume a role in focusing on welfare and poverty as major women's issues. All welfare reform proposals should be examined specifically for their impact on women. Inequality of opportunity for women must be recognized as a primary factor contributing to the growth of welfare rolls.

Women in poverty, whether young or old, want to be part of the mainstream of American life.

Poverty is a major barrier to equality for women.

Millions of women who depend on income transfer programs or low-paying jobs for their basic life support may be subject to the multiple oppression of sexism, racism, and poverty—and they are often old or disabled.

Many other women, because of discriminatory employment practices, social security laws, differential education of men and women, and lack of adequate child care, are just one step away from poverty. Consequently, the elimination of poverty must be a priority of all those working for equal rights for women.

Along with major improvements in the welfare system, elimination of poverty for women must include improvements in social security and retirement systems, universal minimum wage, nontraditional job opportunities, quality child care, comprehensive health insurance, and comprehensive legal services. A concerted effort must be made to educate the public about the realities of welfare, the plight of the blind, the aged, the disabled, and single-parent families and other low-income women.

We support increased Federal funding for income transfer programs (e.g., Social Security, SSI, and AFDC). Congress should approve a Federal floor under payments to provide an adequate standard of living based on each State's cost of living for all those in need. And, just as with other workers, homemakers receiving income transfer payments should be afforded the dignity of having that payment called a wage, not welfare.

We oppose the Carter administration proposal for welfare reform (H.R. 9030), which among other things eliminates food stamps, threatens to eliminate CETA training and CETA jobs paying more than minimum wage, and does not guarantee adequate day care. We oppose proposals for 'workfare' where welfare mothers would be forced to 'work off' their grants, which is work without wage, without fringe benefits or bargaining rights, and without dignity. H.R. 9030 further requires those individuals and families without income to wait weeks, possibly months, before even the inadequate grant is available.

We strongly support a welfare reform program developed from ongoing consultation with persons who will be impacted. This program should: 1) be consistent with the National Academy of Science recommendation that no individual or family living standard should be lower than half the median family income level for substantial periods (after taxes) and that this income should not fall below the Government-defined poverty level of family income even for shorter periods; 2) help sustain the family unit; and 3) insure that women on welfare and other low-income women who choose to work not be forced into jobs paying less than the prevailing wage.

In order to improve the status of women, the following actions should be taken:

a. To insure that welfare and other poor are not discriminated against as an economic class, affirmative action guidelines should be drawn up to provide that all employers who are recipients of Federal and/or State contract monies be required to show that they are hiring recipients.

b. There should be targeting of funds by local CETA advisory boards for the placement and training of women in nontraditional higher paying jobs, consistent with the original mandate.

c. The Department of Labor should make a study of jobs and wages based on a standard of comparable worth and speedily move the implementation of that study in all Governmental positions.

d. Unions should devote additional energy to the organization of women to upgrade pay and working conditions for women in traditional employment.

Quality child care should be a mandated Title 20 service available to all families on an ability-to-pay basis through training, education, job search, and employment.

Congress should encourage education of women by insuring that Federal and other education grants do not reduce an individual's or family's eligibility for public assistance in AFDC or any other program.

Comprehensive support services and social services must be provided and adequately funded.

NOTE ON TERMS

Social Security—a Federal programme of retirement, industrial disability and survivors' payments drawn from a fund of monthly contributions by paid workers and employers.

SSI—Supplementary Security Income. A Federal welfare programme of financial assistance to the 'aged', 'blind' and 'disabled' which is supplemented by individual states.

AFDC—Aid to Families with Dependent Children. A mostly Federally-funded welfare programme which can be supplemented by states and cities, providing financial assistance to 'dependent children' and the relatives with whom they live. It is the key payment to single mothers.

HR 9030—President Carter's 1977 welfare reform bill, which was called The Programme for Better Jobs and Income.

Food stamps—Federally funded food vouchers for low income people.

CETA—Comprehensive Employment and Training Act. A Federal programme providing jobs and job training for the longterm unemployed, mainly in urban areas.

Title 20—of the Social Security Act. A Federal law encouraging states to provide a range of services such as child care, transportation, job training, meals and health support in order to avoid 'dependence' on public financial assistance from AFDC, SSI or Social Security. Neither U.S. citizenship nor longterm residence is an eligibility requirement for Title 20 services.